Tracking The Snow-Shoe Itinerant

Tracking
The Snow-Shoe Itinerant

Photographs by Kent Gunnufson

Text by John Lewis Dyer

A Snowstorm Publication

Acknowledgments

I would like to thank my wife Beth for her help and support. Also I appreciate the generous help of Jerry Keenan, John Shuler, Mark and Roberta Fiester, Kitty Bennett, Kim Rowley, Barbara and Leigh Barksdale. I am grateful to Leslie Feinstein for her patience with all my changes in typesetting.

Library of Congress Catalog Card Number 80-54041

ISBN 0-9605366-0-4   Cloth
ISBN 0-9605366-1-2   Paper

To Melissa

Introduction

By Kent Gunnufson

Up the Colorado River to its headwaters flows the Blue River along the Continental Divide. Summit County is where the mountains reach into the clouds and the majority of the photographs in this text were taken. Here the waters are cold and blue; the air is crisp and clean; and the snow is light and deep. Tremendous snowfalls make this region one of the most desirable for skiing in the world. Snow lies on the ground six to eight months of the year. Temperatures fall to -40 degrees Fahrenheit during some cold winter nights; yet in the summer wildflowers blossom and the alpine valleys bask in the warm sun.

Living in such a dramatic wonderland has instilled in me a strong desire to let others see this beauty. Photographs capture the visual scenes, but I would also like those seeing them to gain a deeper respect and understanding of life in the high country.

The Colorado Rocky Mountains have a rich history of those trying to survive in her environment. In 1861, John Lewis Dyer, a Methodist preacher, came to the Rocky Mountain gold camps. At the age of 49 with his eyes going bad, he walked all the way to Breckenridge, Colorado, from Iowa. He spent a great deal of his life here preaching and helping others. His travels through this majestic land by means of horse, skis, or foot often proved to be a trial for survival. Father dyer lived through ordeals such as avalanches, falling off precipices, and wading across ice-slushed streams barefoot in the winter. A stained glass likeness of Father Dyer is in the Colorado State Capitol as a reminder of his contribution to the state's history. A portion of his autobiography, *SNOW-SHOE ITINERANT*, is represented here to give those reading it an understanding of life during Colorado's gold rush.

Only by experiencing nature's trials can man envision her beauty, persistence, and awesome law. Cognizance of man's struggle with his environment is inherent with mountain life. Father Dyer loved this life as well as its challenge. I welcome anyone who wants to experience the Rocky Mountains to follow me as I track the Snow-Shoe Itinerant.

The Snow-Shoe Itinerant

By John Lewis Dyer

I had make up my mind to see Pike's Peak; that was, if I could see at all, as I had to wet my eyes and wipe them to get them open every morning. I had a bottle of Sloan's Instant Relief that I used every day, and my friends said, "You will put your eyes out on the plains," and advised me not to go. Added to blindness, my means ($14.75) were scanty; but I had made up my mind to go---if I did not starve on the way--and felt that my Heavenly Father would provide, and that my bread and water were sure.

On the ninth day of may, 1861, I left Lenora on a splendid riding animal. Omaha was my first place of destination.

Then, looking at my financial condition, I could see no way out; but I had given all my property up, and had one consolation, and that was, that I had intended to wrong no one, and cared less for what was gone than that I was unable to pay at once all claims against me. I held myself fully committed to pay every cent as soon as I could make it. I rode that day

forty-seven miles. I stopped with a partial acquaintance for the night. We had seen each other several times. I asked for my bill. He looked down his nose, and said, "Twenty-five cents."

From that to Newtown, Iowa, I made fifty miles a day; rested Sunday at the above place. Before eating, I fed and took care of my horse; but while at breakfast, the landlord saw my mare was about to disturb a sitting hen, and took her into another stall where there was a peck of corn. As the result, she was foundered almost to death. I mention this because the hen worth six cents, a dozen of eggs four cents, and his saving ten cents, cost me one hundred and fifty dollars. I led her a few miles and sold her for a gun, an old watch, and fifteen dollars, a very little more than the saddle and bridle were worth.

I stopped a day a Omaha, and there was a train of eighteen wagons starting for Pike's Peak. One of the men agreed to board me across for fifteen dollars, and haul my carpet-sack and gun. I was to walk. We set out for six hundred miles, as it was called. A Mr. Penny bossed the train. We got to Fremont about ten o'clock on Sunday morning. I was told they would have preaching at eleven o'clock. I stayed to hear, and was asked to preach at the afternoon service, and did so. I thought it would be easy to overtake an ox-team, as that was the last settlement between the Missouri River and the Rocky Mountains. I had about thirty hearers. I staid all

"I had made up my mind to see Pike's Peak; that was, if I could see at all, as I had to wet my eyes and wipe them to get them open every morning."

night, and caught up the train.

There were a few soldiers at Fort Kearney. I excercised myself with two or three trips out to the Bluffs, four or five miles. I wanted to see a buffalo, but never got sight of one, much less a chance to shoot one...

We frequently met with Indians. The poor creatures had learned to swear. What a pity the white men had no better manners than to teach them to blaspheme!

One day we came to a station where there were a number of camps, and a lot of drunken men tearing around. A fat dog belonging to the train began to stagger, and soon died. It was thought he got strychnine. The Indians saw him kicking his last, and offered twent-five cents for him. They skinned and cooked him, and soon had dog-soup.

Here a drunken man came into our corral and claimed one of our oxen. Swore he would have him, holding his gun at a ready. I stood at one end to help, and had a big ox-gad. He ran toward me. I raised the gad and told him to get out of there, and made at him, and he got out at the nearest gap. I looked around, and not a man was to be seen; they all were scared. This proved quite a brevet to me.

We reached Julesburg, and there took the cut-off—a new road—which a company had opened, having bridged two or three sand-creeks with poles, and put up a toll-gate, and of course advertised the cut-off. This meant—"Don't follow the Platte River,

and you will soon be in Denver." The trail was not yet worn smoothe, and it seemed long and tedious.

One day, as we were taking our lunch, a German said: "I believes dese cut-offs is one cut-on." It struck us all, for we began to think it about so, since we were all footsore, as well as the oxen, and nothing to break the monotony. The day before we got through, we stopped to water the cattle. I asked my team-boss if I should make some coffee. He was mad, because one of his oxen was not likely to get water, and swore at me. My offer was gratis, for I had not agreed to do any thing, but had done many little things to assist the boys. When I told him he had as well stop his abuse, he said that he did not care for my profession, and would thrash me. Of course I told him he could not do that, and said I did not want to dirty my hands with him, but that he ought to be slapped in the mouth. By this time some of the boys spoke to him, and he shut up. I had got almost through, and had not had a hard word with any of the company. In fact, I believe that, without an exception, they would have defended me to the last, if necessary.

Now we came to the last night on the plains. I had two pairs of pants, about half worn. I had left my pocket-knife and purse in the pocket in the pair that was in the wagon that night, and when I took them out, found the contents all gone. Well, the loss was small, as it was less than two dollars and a-half; but it was all I had, and I

"The next thing I remember was looking toward the house over a small field of wheat. The stalks seemed to be about seven feet high, and the heads nearly a foot long, and they all appeared to be pitching over each other."

was consoled in the fact that I was no worse off than I would have been if it had been five thousand dollars. We stopped two miles up Cherry Creek, above Denver. I took what I had in my carpet-sack, and, with my gun on my shoulder, walked into the town, and met my second son Elias, who had come a year before. He was working in Mr. Sprague's store in West Denver. That was almost all of Denver, the 20th of June, 1861. Suffice it to say, I was surprised to see---so much of a village; and I have seldom, if ever, seen any one since who has not been similarly surprised when he sets his eyes in Denver for the first time. Why should it not surpass his expectation, after traveling six hundred miles across what was called the American Desert, with only here and there a small sod tenement about seven feet high, all at once to come to the metropolis of Pike's Peak?...

I swapped my watch for about twenty dollars' worth of provisions--- flour, side-bacon, dried apples, sugar, coffee, and salt enough to save it, with a few cans of fruit. Price, on an average, about twenty-five cents per pound. My son gave me a buffalo-skin and quilt for bedding. My mind was bent on a mountain trip, and no time to spare, as I thought of getting back by the last of September. The Phillips Lode, at Buckskin Joe, was the point of the greatest excitement at that time. I joined myself to a company which had a team. They hauled my stuff, and I started on foot for another

hundred miles. This was the third day of July, 1861. We reached Apex, at the foot-hills, the first day, which I supposed we would reach by noon. But I was like the man, several years after, that started to the same place before breakfast; traveled till he got tired, and seeing a ditch some fifty yards ahead, he stopped and began to pull off his boots. His comrade asked him what was the matter? He replied; "If that ditch"---about four feet wide---"is as much wider in proportion as the mountains are further from Denver than they look to be, I will have to swim it."

We began to ascend the mountains on the 4th of July, 1861, and as it was my first mountain trip, I was wonderfully interested. It was so different from what I supposed---timber, grass, shrubs of many kinds, strawberry-vines in full bloom, with an occasional view back across the plains. It was a pleasant day. I indulged in reflections on the wonders of the creation of God; but could not conceive that the signers of the Declaration of our Independence had even a faint idea of the half they were doing.

We reached the head of the North Platte, on Kenosha Hill. For over twenty miles, up the canon, we had been shut out from seeing much of the world by the towering mountains on either side. We were well prepared, as we reached the top to be astonished at the sight of South Park, which from this point is a view of grandeur never

"If that ditch (about four feet wide) is as much wider in proportion as the mountains are further from Denver than they look to be, I will have to swim it."

to be forgotten. Prairies, surrounded with high mountains and interspersed with pine-groves and small peaks---a very Eden Park---are a sight seldom surpassed even in the Rocky Mountains.

On the ninth day of July, we reached Buckskin Joe Camp. Just two months from the day I left Lenora, Minnesota, my eyes had improved a little. Otherways, I enjoyed good health, after a tramp of over seven hundred miles on foot...

I now made my way up the range, about eight miles, to the top of the Mosquito Pass, the highest and hardest range I had then crossed. From here I could see the head of the Platte River, Arkansas, Blue River, and the head of the Grand River; like the Garden of Eden, it was at least the starting point of all these mighty rivers.

As I took a view of those gigantic mountain peaks and deep gorges, the thought come to me, if heaven is above, I am nearer Canaan's shores than ever before. After prayer for our country on both sides, and for myself, alone on the dividing range of our great continent, I partook of my frugal stores, and that night preached at California Gulch, now Leadville. The next day started alone for the Gunnison country, following an Indian trail. Had to wade the Arkansas. Took off my boots, and I thought the top of the cold water would cut my legs off; and that I saw for the first time the beautiful Twin Lakes. Had not heard of them

"It was so different from what I supposed--timber, grass, shrubs of many kinds, strawberry-vines in full bloom."

22

before. My surprise may be imagined. My path was up Lake Creek, a perfect mountain wilderness, snowy ranges towering on either side. I had not seen a human being for several miles; night was coming on, and I began to look for a camping-place. I heard, just as the sun was sinking behind the snow-capped mountains, the sound of a bell, and soon found five men. They had one burro to pack their food and blankets. I asked for lodging. They said: "If you can furnish your own accommodations, you can stay." I accepted...

The next day I took my pack and started for Washington Gulch, forty-five miles west, on a dim Indian trail. Near the crossing of Taylor River I overtook a pack-train loaded with food, all but one burro, which had twenty gallons of whisky. Just then we were met by a number of prospectors. They saw the whisky-kegs. Of course they must have some. They caught the burro, one holding it by the head, and another by the tail, and the third trying to get the cork out. The preacher stepped up, and asked if they were tapping the jack. "No," was the reply, "it is the keg." Suffice it to say, they all drank out of a tin cup, and one of them poured out gold-dust into the freighter's hand until he was satisfied. Well, I passed on and for once got in ahead of the whisky.

That day we passed Deadman's Gulch. At this place six white men had been killed by a company of Indians in 1859. It is said that they fought

"We were well prepared, as we reached the top, to be astonished at the sight of South Park, which from this point is a view of grandeur never to be forgotten."

24

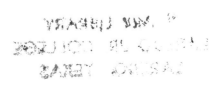

bravely, standing behind their horses; and it looked as though it might have been so, as I saw the bones of several horses, as well as a part of the frames of six human beings, that lay bleaching in the mountains. They had been slightly burried, but the wolves had uncovered them. Kit Carson was informed by the Indians that several of their number were killed, and some wounded. There was none to tell us of the dreadful scene; the tall pines alone witnessed the ascent of the dead men's ghosts.

We camped near that place. It was very high, and disagreeably cold. Next day I camped, in company with two men, in sight of Minersville, on Washington Gulch. Sabbath, the 24th of September, I entered the town, and shall not forget the scene. One man was cutting and selling beef; others rolling logs down the hill; others covering their cabins; another building a chimney; and still others selling provisions and whisky in a tent. From this stand-point I resolved to announce my appointment...

On Tuesday I started back alone on the Indian trail, and near sunset met a German in Deadman's Gulch, and in sight of the bones of the six men killed by the Indians. He made some inquiries. I told him where we were, and pointed to the bones, and he began to whip his jack and put out; did not want to hear any more. Within a mile I met a man that had stopped to camp. We agreed to lodge together. I saw at once that he was a Southerner;

"As I took a view of those gigantic mountain peaks and deep gorges, the thought come to me, if heaven is above, I am nearer Canaan's shores than ever before."

26

his speech betrayed him. I was careful to say nothing relative to the war; but he asked me how I stood as to the Rebellion. I told him I was for the Union, and remarked it would not be worth while for us to fight here, as we had no reporter. He said we could talk friendly on the subject; so we did, and parted friendly, after sleeping under the same tree. He was armed, and I was not, save the arms that God had given me, but I felt safe in his protecting care.

Next day I reached Kent's Gulch, and stayed until Monday...I found room in a cabin to sleep, and after I retired, a man came in and asked me to get up and go with him and marry a couple. Of course I went. I wished to know something of the case in hand.

They gave the following account:

The couple had run away from near Denver. The girl's father was opposed to the match. In their flight, they found a justice, and he performed the ceremony of matrimony. The father followed, with help, some eighty miles; and while the bride and groom were eating their dinner on the bank of a creek in South Park, the pursuing party came up and demanded the girl of sixteen. All being armed, the girl stood between her father and her husband until he hitched up, and then, jumping into the wagon, the plucky couple put for the mountains; and the father and company gave up the chase, but told them he knew the justice had no commission. The groom pleaded with me to marry them, so

"I indulged in reflections on the wonders of the creation of God; but could not conceive that the signers of the Declaration of our Independence had even a faint idea of the half they were doing."

28

that the father would be better satisfied, knowing that a preacher had performed the ceremony. I thought they were married and that it would do no harm to marry them over again, and so did it. I was out of money, and he gave me two half-dollars.

The next day I visited Georgia Bar, on the Arkanas River; found some fifty men at work panning out the dust; gathered a few, and preached at night. Next morning, as I passed up the Bar, thought it a mighty contact, water against rock. I felt gloomy, and the scene looked so; and just as I passed a cabin, a man came out and asked me if I was the man that preached below last night. "Yes, sir." He said a young man died there last night, and asked me to attend the funeral. Forty men and two women were present. All seemed to be deeply affected, as it was the first funeral most of us had been at in the mountains. He was buried as decently as the circumstances would admit. From there I went to California Gulch, and preached; and, after resting a few days, went to the Gunnison again. Falling in with a Mr. Noah Armstrong, we bought a jack, packed him, and though that, as I was on my own hook, it would be well to dig a little, as necessity seemed to demand it.

We prospected over three weeks without success, when a deep snow fell. We were seventy miles from any winter quarters, and the main range to cross, and the snow from three to five feet deep...We were several days on

short allowance, and one day had nothing. We shoveled snow three days and a half to get three and a half miles; but, by the blessing of God, we made the riffle. I reached California Gulch in good health, weighted one hundred and sixty-three pounds, and when I left the States, pulled one hundred and ninety-two pounds. I found out that a man at forty-seven, getting fat, could walk, work, and preach off all the fat.

I stayed at the above place until the 7th of January; held meetings for ten nights; some rose for prayers, but they must have the school-house to dance in, and we had to yield; and then started alone for Buckskin Joe, by the Weston Pass. At timber height I was met by a severe snowstorm. Had a box of matches, but not one would burn. The prospect was frightful. I prayed and dedicated myself to God, and thought that by his grace I would try to pull through. For five or six hours I waded the snow waist-deep, until, almost exhausted, I leaned up against a tree to rest. I never saw death and eternity so near as then. My life seemed to be at an end; but I resolved to keep moving, and when I could go no more, would hang up my carpet-sack, and write on a smooth pine-tree my own epitaph---"Look for me in heaven;" but through the goodness of God, I reached the toll-gate about one hour after dark; and I shall never forget the kindness of the Swede who took me in and cared for me...

In about four months I traveled

near five hundred miles on foot, by Indian trails, crossing logs, carrying my pack, and preaching about three times a week. Received forty-three dollars in collections at different places. Nothing that we ate cost less than twent-five cents per pound, and we had to carry freight on our backs. Spent about fifty dollars of my own resources, as I had worked by the day and job through the week, and preached nights and Sundays. My clothes were worn out; my hat-rim patched with dressed antelope-skin; my boots half-soled with raw-hide. This is a sample of my work and experiences the first year in the mountains of Colorado.

About the 1st of February I started on foot for Denver. We had a stage once a week to Buckskin Joe. Fare, ten dollars each way. I could walk the hundred miles in two days and a half. If I did not make money, I could save some. On Saturday evening I reached the city of Denver, dressed, as far as it went, in miner's clothes, minus a vest...

The next day I was passing a store, and was called in by my esteemed friend, Brother Pease, now of Cheyenne, Wyoming, who made me a present of a vest. I have not been without one since. This gave the colonel a chance to tell an incident, which contrasts the preachers of the past and present, and shows the generosity of a Presbyterian in early times. It was common for our preachers to wear homespun; and

their wives often spun, and sometimes wove the jeans on the common loom. I think they do not do so now...

In the latter part of March, 1862, I received a letter from Brother B.C. Dennis, presiding elder of the Rocky Mountain District, Kansas Conference---at this time Colorado was included in this conference---asking me to take charge of Blue River Mission, Summit County, Colo. I was in Denver, and the next day started on foot. I went by Central City, and the first day out from there it snowed four inches, which made it bad walking. The second day reached Kenosha Hill, remarkably tired. My purse of gold-dust was so light that I feared there would not be enough to pay my bill. I told the landlord that it was possible that my means would not meet my expenses, but wished to stay, and that I would remit to him. He said that it would be all right, and the call for supper soon came. When i sat down, I saw that the food was all cold except a weak cup of tea. After a few mouthfuls, I became sick and left the table, and lay down on a bench in the bar-room and rested, for I was almost given out. After half an hour, another man came in for supper, and while he was eating I went in for a drink of water, and saw hot coffee, ham, and eggs, I thought I would never say anything about pay again until after breakfast, I rested all night, and in the morning ate a hearty breakfast, and gave the host my purse, He weighed out my bill, and I had some left. There were at lest twenty-

five miles to walk, and but one house. I took dinner and handed my purse to the landlord, and he weighed my bill and I crossed the range on a snow-path; for, although it was April, the snow was from five to fifteen feet deep.

I reached Georgia Gulch on the second day of April, and was received kindly. There were about one hundred and fifty people in the Gulch, and I found some few that had been members of some Church. I gave out preaching for the next Sunday at ten and a-half o'clock, and at French Gulch in the afternoon. There was a friendly Jew at Georgia Gulch, who proposed to raise the preacher something, and took a paper and collected $22.50 in dust; for that was all the currency then. This amount was quite

a help, as there were only ten cents in my purse when I got there. There was an appropriation of one hundred and twenty-five dollars from the conference. We had at first five preaching-places for two weeks, and afterwards more.

I saw that what I was likely to get in the new wild country would not board me, as common board was seven dollars a week, and a man had to find his own bed, and do his own washing. I had a chance to buy a cabin in French Gulch or what was then called Lincoln City, and I set up in a humble way keeping bachelor's hall. My bed-stead was made of pine poles, even to the springs. The bed was hay, with blankets for covering. I slept well, and rested as well as though I had

"Kit Carson was informed by the Indians that several of their number were killed, and some wounded. There was none to tell us of the dreadfull scene; the tall pines alone witnessed the ascent of the deadmen's ghosts."

been in a fine parlor-chamber. My furniture was primitive and limited---a table, and a couple of boards against the side of the wall for a cupboard, six tin plates, half a set of knives and forks, with a few other indispensables; a coffee-pot, a tin cup, and a pot for boiling vegetables---when I had them---and a frying-pan. As to a library, mine had not crossed the plains; but we had a few books to read---the Bible, hymn-book, and Methodist Discipline, with two of our weekly *Advocates* and the *Rocky Mountain News*. I tried to keep up with the times.

The compass of my circuit was not large. The farthest appointment was six miles; and I preached about seven times in two weeks. I formed one class, and then discovered that there was little profit in it, as the people stopped so short a time in one place. I concluded to get everybody out, and then preach the truth burning hot, whether my hearers were in the house or around the camp-fire, or, at other times, under the shade of a pine-tree. We generally had good congregations. The way we got them out was to go along the gulches and tell the people in their cabins and saloons where the preaching would be at night, and then, just before the time, to step to the door where they were at cards, and say: "My friends, can't you close your game in ten minutes, and come and hear preaching?" I tried to adapt my-self to the situation, neither showing that I felt above anyone, nor ever com-promising with sin or with transgres-

sions, and being ready always to speak for the Lord Jesus Christ.

We cooked by a fire-place, generally baking our bread in a frying-pan set up before the fire. I must not forget to say that we had stools and benches in place of chairs. There was one chair left in my house, made by some one out of crooked pine-limbs, with the seat of ropes. It was so comical that if I had it now, I would certainly place it in an exposition. It was easy enough for an editor.

I tried to make my cabin useful. It was about eighteen feet square, and, taken every way, the best place to hold our meetings. The floor was hard ground. I got gunny-sacks and made carpet...

The first county officers had been elected the fall previous, and the assessor refused to act, and it was intimated that he was afraid that the miners would not stand it to be assessed; so he, with others, insisted that I should take the office as deputy. I told them the office I held was all I could attend to, and that I did not wish to take the responsibility. But they were set on my doing the work, and I concluded to try. Only one man resisted me, and I made him believe that he was the best man I could get to help me, if there was any resistance. He asked me to dinner, and ever after was one of my warmest friends. When I was through, I charged them fifty dollars, and got it after two years; and it came in good time, as I was then in a close place.

"Just as I got on top of the Hoosier Pass it began to snow."

42

My appointments were Park City (Georgia Gulch), American Gulch, Galena Gulch, Delaware Flats, Gold Run, Lincoln City, Mayo Gulch, and Breckenridge. It was a two weeks' circuit. I preached once at least in Gibson Gulch, and I must say that we had, without an exception, good behavior and good attention. Although we all looked rough, the miners treated me and the cause of Christ with respect. Often after preaching I was greeted warmly, and some of them would say the service reminded them of home. They were generally liberal, although it was not the custom always to pass the hat, and sometimes the preacher, when his pants began to wear out, would think the boys rather long between collections. It was common to give a dollar all around; and to this day I would as soon ask miners for help, with assurance of receiving, as any class of men I have ever found. They were always ready to divide, although at times they would take exceptions to a man that wore a plug hat or noticeably fine clothes.

I made me a pair of snow-shoes, and, of course, was not an expert. Sometimes I would fall; and, on one occasion, as I was going down the mountian to Gold Run, my shoes got crossed in front as I was going very fast. A little pine-tree was right in my course, and I could not turn, and dare not encounter the tree with the shoes crossed; and so threw myself into the snow, and went in out of sight.

This was my regular round on the

circuit. We had a new field, one that gave a good chance to read human nature, in the fastnesses of the Rocky Mountains, where moral and reigious restraints were absent. The most of the men would go to the bar and drink, and play at cards, and the Sabbath was a high day for wickedness. Balls were the common amusement, especially in winter. The women were as fond of this as the men. Although far in the minority, they were accosted like this: "Now, Miss, or Mistress, you must surely come, as we can't have a set or cotillion without you". Often the father was left with the children at home; at other times both went and took the children; and then the old bachelors would hold the baby so that the mother could dance every set.

I will give an instance at Lincoln City, at our hotel. They must give a Christmas dinner, and, of course, a dance at night. I concluded to take dinner with them. The host made me no charge, as it would be what we old bachelors called a square meal. As I was about to leave, the ladies pleasantly invited me to stay to the dance. Of course I could not accept the invitation. But they said: "You visit at our houses, and you ought to show us respect and stay." At the last came the lady of the house, and said: "This is an extra occasion, and it will be no harm for you to dance with me; why can't you accept my offer?" The reply was "You're a lady, but not quite handsome enough for me to dance with". She was taken back at that, and

the others laughed, and I got out, as my cabin was only two hundred feet away. They soon fiddled me to sleep. But they danced till daylight, and often drank at the bar. Being full, and having no place to sleep, they went up to Walker's saloon. He made some hot sling, and that set them off. The declared that every man in town must get up, and the preacher should treat the company or make a temperance speech. It was just daylight when we heard them on the street, and as they had always passed me before, I turned the key and hoped they would do so again. But when they found the door fast they said: "If you don't open it we ill break it in." I threw it open and invited them in; but they said: "We have come to take you up to Walker's,

and you can either treat or make a temperance speech." I requested them to let me eat breakfast first; but they said: "You must go now." I slipped out, leaving the door open, and went ahead of the company.

Soon they were over forty men, and they called a chairman or moderator; but they were too drunk to be moderated. I got upon a box and stated my arrest, and proposed to make the speech. They said: "Go on." I said: "Gentleman, first I will tell you what I think! There is not a man here but would be ashamed for this father, mother, sisters, or brothers, to know just our condition here this morning." They stamped and roared out, "That's so," all over the house, "and next," I continued, "if we were

not so drunk, we would not be here," (Cheers, "That's so, too!" all over the house,) "And if we were a little drunker, we could not do as we are now doing." (Cheers and "That's so!" all over the house.) I wound up and was about to take leave, but the judge said: "I move that we vote that every thing Mr. Dyer has said is true;" and they gave a rousing vote. He said, "The ayes have it," but that I must not go yet; and made and put a motion that they all give Mr. Dyer one dollar apiece; and that was also carried. They took the hat, got twenty dollars, and I thanked them and went home to breakfast.

As all the mining was gulch or placer diggings, a great part of the people left in the fall to winter---some for Denver, others for Canon City or Colorado City, some crossing the Missouri River with ox-teams. Only a few would come back in the spring; for men did not come to Pike's Peak---as it was called---to stay, but to make a raise, and then go back...

In March, 1863, I received my appointment from Kansas Conference, my work up to this time had been as a supply. Through the presiding elder, L.B. Dennis, I was readmitted. It was a surprise, for I had not made up my mind to stay in the mountains. This decided me to stand the storms and leave the events with God, and do the best I could to build up the Church in this wilderness country. I was put down for South Park, and on the third day of April left

Lincoln City and stopped at Mr. Silverthorn's, in Breckenridge, until about two o'clock in the morning, when I took my carpet-sack, well filled, got on my snow-shoes, and went up Blue River. The snow was five feet deep. It might be asked, "Why start at two o'clock?" Because the snow would not bear a man in daytime, even with snow-shoes. From about two o'clock until nine or ten in the morning was the only time a man could go; and a horse could not go at all. When about three miles up the Blue River, back of McCloud's, the wolves set up a tremendous howling quite near. I was not armed, but passed quietly along, and was not disturbed. It was not likely, I thought, that the Good Lord would let anything disturb a man going in the night to his appointment, although wolves and bears, with some Rocky Mountain lions, were numerous.

I reached Montgomery about nine o'clock in the morning. The snow drifted above the tops of the doors. All along the streets steps had been make in the snow, and served as stairs to get into the stores and houses. There were some two or three hundred people in town, among them seven members. I must mention Brother and Sister Gurton, and Brother and Sister Fowler. I stayed eight days, and held service each evening; on Sunday twice. Two or three professed to be reclaimed, and we all were revived. My circuit embraced the above, with Buckskin Joe, Mosquito, Fair Play,

"They had been a year or two in the gorges of the mountains in search of gold, and had spent all they brought across the Plains from their homes."

and Tarryall. Buckskin Joe was so called from the nickname given to a prospector wearing a suit of that material.

Tarryall was discovered in 1860. Some very rich claims were opened, and soon all were taken. The news spread, and prospectors by the thousands came, but with no chance to get a foot of ground; so they all tarried, and hence the name Tarryall. From there the prospectors went every way, and some struck pay dirt in the Platte, and called it Fair Play, as they claimed to be more liberal.

Mosquito got its name from this circumstance: The miners met to organize. Several names were suggested, but they disagreed, and a motion was made to adjourn and meet again, the place for the name to be left blank. When they came together on appointment, the secretary opened the book, and a large mosquito was mashed right in the blank, showed it, and all agreed to call the district Mosquito...

In 1863...about Midwinter, I found myself without means, and so sought work, but could get none, unless I would work on Sundays, which was out of the question when necessary, except to prevent actual starvation.

In the forepart of February, a man came to me who had the contract to carry the mail from Buckskin Joe to Cache Creek by Oro, California Gulch, a distance of thirty-seven miles. He had carried it as long as he could on a

mule. It was once a week, and he offered me eighteen dollars a week to carry it on snow-shoes. I thought at once: "I can preach about as often as I have been doing, and am not obliged to go on Sunday." So I took the mail, and crossed the Mosquito Range every week, and preached three times a week.

Right here let me tell how I came out. This was wartimes, and the currency was greenbacks. In California Gulch and Cache Creek they were drifting out gold-dust all winter. Gold was on the rise, so that an ounce of dust brought over forty dollars in greenbacks, and so I added exchange to my business and became expressman, and got the per cent agreed on. One man gave me five dollars each time, and I carried all he had to send. At one time I had enough dust to bring in Denver thirty-seven hundred dollars in currency. Suffice it to say, I made over three times more expressing than my wages for mail-carrying. I boarded myself, or paid my board, received forty dollars on the circuit, and at the end of five months, had twelve hundred dollars...This was the first year of my itinerancy that I made any money...

Now for some of the incidents in the mail-service. The mail's weight was from twenty-three to twenty-six pounds, with from five to seven pounds of express matter. The carriage was on snow-shoes, over an Indian trail that was covered from three to twenty feet with snow. My

snow-shoes were of the Norway style, from nine to eleven feet in length, and ran well when the snow was just right, but very heavy when they gathered snow. I carried a pole to jar the sticking snow off. Suffice it to say that the winter of 1863 and 1864 was a remarkably hard one, and the spring held on until June, with terrible snow-storms. I was the first to cross the Mosquito Range with a horse. That was the third day of July. I carried a shovel, but did not have to use it. The mailbags went the trip across and back every week. I had for two weeks a substitute. There was no cabin from Mesquito to California Gulch, and no one living between the Gulch and Cache Creek. At first I had no company, say the first month. After that I often went in the night, as it thawed in the day so that it was impossible to travel, and passengers sought to go with me. A man came up from Denver, and we had a hard trip. He begged me to stop. On top of the range he lay down to sleep, and it was with difficulty that I could get him up. I knew that if he went to sleep, chilled as we were, he would never awake until the judgement. We finally reached Oro City at breakfast-time. That man was one of the leaders of a mob that caused the death of a number of better men than he was. One of his victims was my son.

Again, I was coming over, and at the foot of the pass, at the head of Evans Gulch, I overtook two men. One, an old man, was given out. I saw at

once that it was death with him without a desperate effort. It was seven miles back, and farther ahead, to a house, and the wind piercingly cold. It seemed impossible to make him believe he could walk either way. The snow and wind were blowing so that a man could hardly stand. I determined to get him over the range and down as far as the timbers, and build a fire and keep him from freezing. We told him what could be done, and he would not even try to get on his feet. I took hold of him, and when he was about half up his hat blew off, and the last I saw of it, it was about thirty feet up, and the wind making sport with it. He had on a soldier's overcoat, and as the hat went off the cape blew over his head. We tied it fast with a handerchief. He had taken off one of his gloves, and it was so frozen he could not get it on. I gave him a mitten, took his arm, and got him about three hundred feet up the mountain, and he sat down. I went back and got the mail-sack and his and my snow-shoes. The snow was so packed one the west side of the range that we carried our shoes. I passed him three hundred feet, laid them down, and went back and helped him up, and when we got to the load, he sat down, and I carried them as much further and helped him to the top, which was a mile and a quarter, and said to him: "Now you shall walk alone." He started, and after going a few yards, he said: "Anybody can walk down-hill." Suffice it to say, we all got into Mosquito by nine o'clock. The old

"Many grew home-sick when they found that they could not pick up the gold, and left."

60

man's fingers and ears were frosted a little. He was going to Montana, and said, if he struck it big, he would remember me. As I have never heard from him, I suppose he had poor luck.

Again, there were three men---one was Dr. Hewett, a friend and acquaintance; another a boy about sixteen years old. As the men were not used to such trips, I took pains to go slowly until we reached the top of the range. The boy complained of cold. I kept my course to the pass, as it was in the night, by the slope of the mountain, and stopped several times, and waited a little until I could see or hear them coming. The boy said he was cold, and they could take care of themselves. We saw them no more, but thought they were coming, as one of them had been

over before; but they lost the course, and the doctor missed his footing and slid down the mountain about three hundred feet, to a bench that had caught considerable fresh snow, and enabled him to stop. If he had gone twenty feet further, he would have been carried five hundred feet to the gorge below. His two companions stood just where he started, and called loudly for him. He heard them, but was unable to make them hear. He shot off his pistol and they succeeded in making a connection, got safely to Bird's-eye Gulch, and next day at noon reached Oro City, hungry and weary.

I was very uneasy. I arrived with my boy by three o'clock, took a sleep, and, about one hour before they got in, started with a man to the range, to try,

if possible, to find them; for I feared something had befallen them. But we could not even find their tracks, as the wind had covered them with snow. So I went back to Mesquito; heard nothing of them, and told where they left me. The news got back to Denver. The friends of one of them were preparing for a funeral, when they heard, to their great joy, of their safety.

Another time, for some cause, the stage failed for a week to come from Denver, and the next time we had two weeks' mail, and four passengers bound for California Gulch; and we were obliged to go mostly in the night, while the snow was solid. At the hotel, while at dinner, the passengers inquired for the mail-carrier, and I was pointed out to them. One, an Irishman, said: "Is this Mr. Dyer?" "Yes, sir." "Well we are glad to see you. We want to go over, and we wouldn't go with anybody else, as we have been told you are so well acquainted with the range." "Be assured I am glad to have the company of four such strong young men, as I have two sacks to take over; and if you join together, it will be easy for you to carry one, and I will guide you all safe over." He at once stopped his blarney, but the others were willing to accept the proposition; but as soon as dinner was over, the Irishman began to make fun of his comrades; said he would not carry the mail, and could go just as well as anybody, and that they did not need a guide. In due time we all set out, and he took the path ahead for three miles,

"To this day I would as soon ask miners for help, with assurance of receiving, as any class of men I have ever found. They were always ready to divide, although at times they would take exceptions to a man that wore a plug hat or noticeably fine clothes."

until he got to the crossing of the creek. He undertook to cross on a pole, but fell, and came near falling into the water. He got up, and started to find another place to cross. We all crossed over safely, and he had to come back to get over. By that time we were ahead of him, and the trail was hard to see. He got lost, and cried aloud. I answered him, but we kept on, and when he came up he was all in a sweat. There was a brother Irishman along, who said: "Now you have got to carry this mail-sack." He was willing enough. Just above timber, we had about one mile of snow, say six inches deep, and water under. He wore shoes, and his feet got wet, and it was freezing cold. When we got to the steep part of the mountain, he asked me to wait until he could change his socks, as his feet were wet. He made the charge, and we had gone but a short distance until he began to cry, and said, he was a ruined man, that his feet were frozen---"Boo-hoo! boo-hoo!"---and a little further on he threw himself down on the snow, and said he would not have come for a thousand dollars; that his feet were ruined. He cried and prayed, and said, if his friends only know where he was and how he suffered! I told his comrade to pull him up on his feet, and make him come along, or he would perish. He took his hands, and raised him, while he was crying like a boy of five years' old, and said to him: "What the d--l do you want your friends to know? I don't want mine to know where I am!" and so he led the man

"Although we all looked rough, the miners treated me and the cause of Christ with respect."

66

who "could go as well as anybody, without a guide." We got over, and down to the nearest timber, and built a fire. When he came up, his friend took his shoes and socks off, and said: "Your feet are not hurt--they are as red as a turkey-gobbler's gills." The poor fellow sobbed and cried clear across, with his feet aching, but not frozen. We got both sacks of mail through by three o'clock in the morning, and felt pleased to have a sack carried; and the music, crossing the range, even yet prompts a smile.

We will close this account of our mail-service by mentioning two or three lonely trips. Once, leaving Mosquito at two o'clock in the morning in a snow-storm, when near timber height, plodding our way on deep snow, all of a sudden I felt a jar, and the snow gave way under me, and a noise struck my ear like a death-knell. I thought it was a snow-slide, and turned as quickly as possible up the mountainside. About a hundred and fifty feet ahead, I came to a crack six inches wide, and the snow had settled about six inches. It will easily be believed that I felt better on the upper side of the break. A week after, there was a snow-slide right from that break that filled the gorge below.

At sunrise I was near the summit of the range, very weary, and sat down under a large rock. I looked through the snow-storm to the east. The sun rose clear, but across South Park the wind was furious and full of snow. The sun penetrated the storm so that the

"Prospectors thought nothing of shoveling five feet of snow to start a shaft."

68

wonders could be clearly seen. While the wind was blowing the snow from the northwest, there would small whirls start low down, and rising, grow larger, until they would be of enormous size. The main storm passed between them as though they were not connected, even as the mighty current flows past the whirlpool in the water. Although my situation was very disagreeable, I could stop a few minutes and gaze at this astonishing Rocky Mountain scene, sitting in the storm to watch its wondrous ways.

Soon after this I started earlier; but is proved to be too much so, for when I reach the other side of the range, there was snow for two miles, and it would not quite bear me. Some-times I would go three steps and sink to the waist in the snow, and then three steps before I could get on top again. It made the situation very serious. About midnight, after reflection, not fearing human hands, and believing that the wild beasts would have more good manners than to touch it, I set up the mail-sack on the end in the snow, and made for the nearest timber off to the north, as I had seen a small spot of bare ground there when I passed before. But how to get there! Well, I rolled and crawled until I reached the timber, where I pushed over a dry stump, and soon had a fire to warm by. I had time for thanksgiving and prayer, even if I had no supper. Cutting some pine-boughs, I made a bed and took a sleep,

and it was daylight when I awoke. My first thought, after thanking God that I was as safe there in his hands as anywhere, was whether it had frozen so that I could walk. I started, and had not gone more than three steps when I went down to the waist. I knew it was softer near the edge. I crawled up and tried again, and it bore me. It was hardly fair light when I reached the mail-sack, found it just as I left it; the wolves had discovered it and gone within about ten feet of it, and had walked around it until they had beaten quite a path in the snow, but never touched it. It is worthy of note that the mail-carrier had an appetite when he reached Oro City!

We come now to the last incident. I left California Gulch about the middle of March. It was thawing, with alternate snow and sunshine, until about one o'clock. The snow stuck to my shoes so that traveling was very heavy. None but those who have tried snow-shoes when the snow sticks to them can understand how soon it will tire a man down, knocking the snow off at every step. It was so this time. When within a few hundred feet of the pass at the head of Evans Gulch, I looked to the north and saw a black cloud just coming over. The wind that preceded it gave evidence of its terror. No pen or tongue can describe its awful appearance. I fastened and tied up my neck and ears, and took its bearings with reference to my course up the mountain, about how it would strike me, so that I might keep my

"Look to the mountains, for there the treasures are abundant and unfailing."

72

course in the snow. But when the storm struck me, I could not have stood up had I not braced against my snow-shoes, which I had taken off and held in position for that purpose. I had thought I could keep my course by the bearings of the storm, but when it struck me, it was in a perfect whirl, and I had nothing left but the shape of the mountains, and by this time the snow was so dense that it appeared to be a white wall within ten feet in any direction.

I found myself unable to make more than fifty yards before resting, and had to hold my hand over my mouth and nose to keep the snow out so that I could breathe, bracing with my snow-shoes in order to stand. On the west side the snow all blew off, so that I had to carry my shoes. About the third stop, I came to a large rock, and braced against it; and in the midst of the awful surroundings, poured out my soul to God for help, and felt encouraged to try, in his name, to make the trip. I could not travel against the wind, so I had to bear to the right, which brought me on the range south of the old Indian trail, where there was no way to get down without goint over a precipice. I hoped that the wind would abate, so that I might make the trail. But I could not see anything in the whirling snow. It took by breath, and I concluded to retrace by steps; for I felt that to stay there or go forward was equally to perish. I made a desperate effort, but started east instead of west. I had gone

scarcely three rods when my foot slipped off the precipice. I threw myself back in the snow. The air was so thick with snow that I could not see how it was. I could not tell whether the pitch was ten feet or fifty. The cold wind seemed to be feeling for my heart-strings, and my only chance for life was to let myself go over. I took my long snow-shoes, one under each arm, holding the crooked end in each hand for rudders, and believed that if I could thus keep my feet foremost, I could go down alive. I said, "O God, into thy hands I commit my soul, my life, my all; my faith looks up to thee;" and then, with composure, I let go; and, as might be expected, there was a great body of new, soft snow for me to fall in. I have never been certain how far it

was. It was soon over, and I was buried in six or eight feet of new snow that had just blown over. My heels struck the old snow, which must have pitched at an angle of more than forty-five degrees, and my weight carried me, and according to former desires, my feet were foremost, and I went at railroad speed. My snow-shoes must keep me straight. I was covered with snow from the start. I raised my head so that I could breathe, and when I had got near one-half mile, I began to slack up, as I had passed the steepest part, and soon stopped.

I now discovered that I was on the horse-shoe flat between the range and the timber on Mosquito Creek. I got up, but could not see ten feet, the snow was so thick. But I knew if I kept down

the mountain, I would come out all right. Putting on my snow-shoes, I soon came to timber. The first tree was the top of a large pine, standing just at the foot of a precipice. It was well that I saw it in time to turn my course. I took down Mosquito Creek. The snow covered almost all the willows and brush, and the wind pressed me so that for rods there was no need of taking a step. My shoes ran like skates. The snow began to abate, but darkness was closing in on me.

When I was within one mile of my cabin, I saw a pool of water in the creek; and as I had been fearful for some time that my feet were frozen, I thought of Job when his sons had been out frolicking; he sacrificed for them for fear they had sinned. But it looked rather rough to go in over my boots in order to draw the frost out, when I still had hopes that my feet were not frozen. I reached my lonely cabin, started a fire, and my feet began to hurt. I soon had them in the spring, and held them awhile, but it was too late to cure. I got my supper, but did not sleep much. Next morning an old brother, whom everybody called "Uncle Tommy Cummings," brought a little balsam sapling, and we shaved off the bar, and poulticed both of my feet. The third week I was able to carry mail. Half my toe-nails sloughed off, with considerable of the skin. For two weeks I was confined to the house, busying myself reading and doctoring my feet. I sent to H.A.W. Tabor, our store-keeper---now ex-senator---and

"Winter was approaching...I had not more than half enough to carry me through."

78

paid him sixteen cents a pound for corn to make hominy, which I considered a luxury.

Our provisions were all drawn over the plains with teams of cattle, mules, and horses. We had some sharp fellows that made a corner on flour about this time, and the price was forty dollars a sack. Fortunately, I had one sack on hand in Buckskin Joe. My friends in Californis Gulch were out, and wished me to supply them. I tried to buy a pack-pony, but could only find a pack-cow, which I purchased and packed, and tied to a post while I ate breakfast.

An old friend, Mr. Moody, volunteered to help me start. We tied a long rope around her horns about the middle, and he took the lead, and I drove. The cow got on the war-path, and bawling, took after him on a down grade. He ran as fast as he could, and I held as well as I could; and the cow jumped as high and as far as she could. The old man did his best, and the old cow would light right at him every jump. Finally he took round the corner, and she after him. Just then the cingle broke, and the pack-saddle with the flour went down right behind her. Then, lack-a-day! she stopped, and did just as cows do when they are about played out.

After this novel scene I gave up the idea of trying to feed the hungry with temporal bread, and confined myself to dispensing the bread of life. Some ministers may say that the above was hardly becoming; but the

alternative was, either to leave the work and conference, or earn a living, and I was not educated up to the point that a man is justified in leaving if the people do not pay a good salary...

I spent the winter traveling on snow-shoes preaching on an average four times a week. I had a cabin, which I called home, at Mosquito; the post-office being called Sterling. I cut my own wood, and had an old-fashioned fireplace to sit by; a few books to read; a bedstead made of poles, and a bed made of the tops of fir-trees, and finished out with a hay tick---a very comfortable outfit. There was one window, containing six panes of glass, ten by twelve inches, affording plenty of light, except on stormy days, when it was neccessary to keep the door open, if the wind would allow. I could enjoy the hospitality of friends at my various appointments, but when I got around I wanted some place that I could call home. The above was my home, or answered that purpose. How glad I was to get back, stand my snow-shoes up against the house, strike up a fire, sit down, and warm a little; and then, if there was not any bread to warm up, and satisfy my hunger, to take flour and baking-powder, and make a delicious cake! I generally baked it in a frying-pan before the fire. By the time it was baked, the meat was fried, coffee boiled, and with a can of fruit or some dried-apple sauce, the table was set, and I was ready to thank God and eat!...

That spring---May 20th (1867)---I

took stage from Fair Play to Denver. I got as far as Hamilton---just above Como---all right. There were some five passengers in all; Mr. Cy. Hall---the rich and clever Denverite of to-day---driver. I was in the front seat. Mr. Hall said: "You sit back, and let Billy Berry sit here; he knows the road better than any of us." It had already begun to snow, and the old packed snow was about two feet deep. The horses and sled sunk about six inches. It snowed almost straight down, and was foggy. We had not gone more than a mile till we lost the road. It was about four miles to Michigan Ranch, and we traveled all day till near sundown. We knew the creek ahead, and Tarryall Creek behind, and a hill on each side, and in all this time never saw either. It

looked as though we were elected to make a hotel of ourselves. Unexpectedly we heard the report of a gun a mile away. We answered with strong voices, and made toward the sound. We got in about sundown, and stopped for the night.

Next morning, before we got to Brubaker's Ranch, crossing a slough, the water had begun to run under and over the snow. Right in the middle the horses went down, and the water almost ran over them. It looked as though they would drown. Mr. Hall got to the first span, but most of the passengers were a little sick just then. However I worked out to the leaders, and kept their heads out of the water until we got them loose from the sled, in which sat three men quietly look-

"The sun penetrated the storm so that the wonders could be clearly seen."

84

ing on till we got all the horses out. We took a long rope and tied to the tongue, hitched the horses, and pulled out. We stopped at Hank Farnham's to warm. I was wet to the waist with snow-water. This was staging---sledding, in fact---almost the last of May...

When I came into the mountain, in 1861, Lake county included all the territory west of Park county. My first visit was in July of that year, I was well acquainted with its mountains and gorges as far as Gunnison, and equally well acquainted with the early settlers. To say the least, they were a fair specimen of miners in the early days of Colorado. I believe I had their general good-will as I preached to them. I felt at home among them, and, indeed, called it home from 1866 to 1868,

during which time I helped to get some settlers into the lower part of the county. It must be remembered that Chaffee County has been taken off since. In 1867 I was elected probate judge of the county. I did not want the office for honor or profit; but the majority of the people called me to it. I served them about one year, and then resigned, having been sent by the conference to New Mexico.

I had reason to respect many of the citizens. Few professed anything but to take the world as it came, and that generally proved to be a very rough way. Below the Twin Lakes the settlers were mostly ranchmen. All seemed to go along fairly; but talebearing, a lie once in awhile, landclaims and surveying land, in some

cases entering land fraudulently, irrigating ditches---the depraved heart, full of covetousness, made great use of all these to stir up strife. Out of very trivial causes great dissensions sometimes arose. I mention one case, because it led up to the murder of my son: Mr. Elijah Gibbs, a very straightforward man, moved into the neighborhood. The disposition of the older settlers was to domineer over the new-comers. If they submitted, all right; if not, then there were means to subdue their haughty spirits. So when Mr. Gibbs drove up and tied his team where a gang were threshing, he was soon astonished at seeing his team hitched to the machine, his permission having neither been asked nor granted. He indignantly and, I fear, profanely ordered his team put back, under pains and penalties. From then on there was bad blood between these parties, aggravated by conflicting land and water claims. Mr. Gibbs and Mr. Harrington quarreled over a ditch in which they were jointly interested. Almost a pitched battle ensued, but neither was hurt. That night somebody set fire to Mr. Harrington's out-house. He got up, and ran out to extinguish the fire, and was shot and killed by some person unknown. There is no question but that whoever did the dasdardly deed should have been hung. The circumstances of the previous quarrel pointed suspicion at Gibbs. As soon as the word went out, a party gathered and went to hang him. But he and

some of his friends were armed, and declared that it could not be done; but that if they wished to try the law they could do so; and if Gibbs was found guilty, justice would be permitted to take its course.

A warrant was taken out, and he was tried and acquitted. He went back and went to work on his ranch, intending to live the suspicion down; but those who first went to hang him, to the number of fifteen, filled themselves with strong drink, went to his cabin, and ordered him to come out and be hung like a man. Gibbs was alone, except his wife and little children, and a neighbor woman with her little child; but his courage and presence of mind did not desert him. Barring the door, he prepared to defend himself. His besiegers piled brush against the back of the house and fired it, to drive him out. The result not being satisfactory, using Gibb's favorite race-horse as a shield, they made another pile against the door. Through a hole at the side of the door Gibbs saw what was going on, and realized the imminence of his peril. When one of his assailants struck a match to fire the pile, he opened with his revolver on the crowd, shooting two men. A third was wounded, but with shot. As no shot-gun was discharged from within, it is likely that in the excitement outside a gun was accidentally fired, with the result stated above.

Discovering a man at the back of the house climbing on to the yard-

fence, he shot at him through the window. He heard the ball strike, and thought it hit his pistol-scabbard, and that the man was one of the leaders. It turned out, however, to be a man who lived with one of the leaders, and he was wounded in the fleshy part of the hip. I believe this man recovered; but the other three died in about three days, two brothers and an uncle. I heard they expressed sorrow for the course they had taken, and said they did not blame Gibbs for the defense of his family.

The excitement was past discription. Gibbs's friends thought it best for him to leave. So, with two or three others, he started. But his would-be murderers collected and pursued him, bound to take him dead or alive.

Gibbs's party made their escape through the mountains---sometimes hearing their pursuers---to Monumemt, where they had acquaintances, with whom they left their horses, and took the cars for Denver.

When Gibbs's baffled pursuers went back, they formed what they called a Committee of Safety!--after they had got three men killed and one wounded. Everybody said that Gibbs had done just right in defending himself, and that if he had killed more of them it would have been well. The press of the Territory also sustained him. This "Committee of Safety" gathered all they could on their side, including a lot of tie-cutters, some sixty men all told. They seized horses to ride, and they arrested all who did

not think or do and say as they did. Head-quarters were at Nathrop's mills. As the suspects were brought in, the committee questioned them as to their opinion whether Gibbs murdered Harrington. This was all the reason they claimed for their tyrannical procedure.

Among those hauled up was my son, Probate Judge E.F. Dyer. They acted roughly with him; asked if he believed Gibbs shot Mr. Harrington, etc. He told them he did not. When he was forty miles away at work, he heard that Gibbs had done it; but had then said that he could not and would not believe it unless it was proven on him. He had known Gibbs every since 1860, and firmly believed that he was innocent of the crime alleged against him.

Of course the "committee" were furious. He had a pistol on his person, and could have used it, but determined that he would not unless his life were in danger.

A notice, signed by order of the committee, to leave within three days and to resign his office, was served on him; but as they had taken his horse, and as he could not walk in the snow by reason of a stiff knee from white-swelling, he did not obey. So the second time they brought him before their august presence. He insisted on the return of his horse, and finally they brought it, and he started. A few miles out, as he was going up a gorge, he was stopped by a guard of two armed men. Their orders were to let no

"We prospected over three weeks without success, when a deep snow fell. We were seventy miles from any winter quarters, and the main range to cross, and the snow from three to five feet deep."

94

one come out or go in on that road. One of them had been befriended by him, and gave him permission to go to Granite. He headed in that direction, but soon turned toward Fair Play, avoiding the road for some miles. It was hard traveling, as the snow was deep, and the weather cold, in mid-winter. Some time in the night he reached Fair Play. Thence he went to Denver, and visited us at Monument.

The mob of safety procured government arms, and ran off about forty of the inhabitants. It was their gentle policy, when their prisoners would not answer the questions satisfactorily, to hang them awhile in order to subdue their refractory spirits. One of their victims, a Mr. Marion, I saw while his neck was yet sore. Some had

to leave home and property, some stock on the range. One or more women died from the terrible excitement. A Mr. Hardin, the outspoken proprietor of a pack-train, cursed their infamous conduct, and was soon thereafter found by the roadside murdered, together with his dog, whose paw the ruffians had clasped in the dead man's hand.

And all this where there were laws, and courts, and officers to prevent such outrages, or to punish their perpetrators! But it appeared that judge, governor, constable, sheriff, like Gallio, "cared for none of these things." I had a talk with the governor, and asked him to send men to put a stop to such proceedings. He intimated that he had heard from the

"A perfect mountain wilderness, snowy ranges towering on either side."

96

other side, and paid no attention to my plea. I said, "Governor, if you won't do anything to stop such a state affairs, I am keen to tell you that I have no use for such a governor, and our country has much less use," and left him. I concluded that it was a political dodge, and that he wanted to be on the strongest side, even at the price of not fulfilling the obligations of the highest office in the Territory. The mob carried all before them, and always managed to have a grand jury that was on their side.

At the first meeting of our representatives, I thought to get a bill passed to attach Lake to some other county for judicial purposes. I went to as many as three Republicans to help me after the governor refuse. They either wished to be excused, or refused outright to take a hand in it. I felt that I had some claim for help in such a time of distress and violation of laws; but I got the cold shoulder I met Judge Miller. He was aquainted with the case; said he would draw the bill, for he believed E.F. Dyer was a part of the government. After having been refused by my own party, I met Mr. Andy Wilson, a Democrat, and he took the bill, and at the proper time, presented it. As soon as it was filed, a delegation came down from Lake and defeated it. This was from the upper end of the county, before Leadville's boom, when the county was weak. Not many of them had anything to do with the mob, but did nothing to stop it. When it took such proportions, they,

"At sunrise I was near the summit of the range, very weary, and sat down under a large rock."

98

or most of them, would rather let murder go unpunished than to saddle the feeble county with the expense of prosecuting the offenders. And as soon as news of the defeat of the bill got to Oro, a meeting was called and Mr. H.A.W. Tabor's store, the largest house there; and resolutions were adopted commending S.Y. Mashall and others for the defeat of the "infamous" and "nefarious" act!

Of those connected with the mob, so many have died suddenly or been killed, either by their own hands or the hands of others, that I have heard even wicked men say that it looked as if the Almighty had followed the guilty with his judgments.

After Harding and others had been shot down, the governor sent out General Dave Cook, a detective. A Mr. John McPherson, who had a clubfoot, and did not go around with the mob, but wrote letters to papers in their defense, justifying them, was able to be of great service to them, by pouring oil on the troubled waters, and contributing to the impression made on General Cook's mind that, as everything had quieted down, well enough were best left alone. Whether money was used I do not pretend to say. Some affirmed that while the leaders were manipulating the detective for a favorable report, Uncle Jesse Marion, whom they held in custody, and whom they had hung once or twice, managed to give his guards---who were so much interested in the conference with Cook, that they left him

"The snow had covered everything; and as I passed over some willows, I broke one of my shoes; but got to the ford, and saw that there was no way to cross but by wading."

100

for a few minutes---the slip, and taking down the Arkansas River, made his escape. I saw him after he got to the valley. His neck was yet sore from the rope. He seemed to think Mr. Cook would not have been so ready to report favorably if it had been his own neck that was sore.

As to Mr. McPherson's accusations about Brown's Creek, and the dishonesty that had been unearthed there by those who had been engaged in setting fire to a house over women and little children, and in killing men and hanging others to make them tell what they wanted told,---they are not worth notice. How the governor could reconcile his apathy whilst this lawlessness continued---during which ten or twelve were killed outright, and a whole country terrorized--with his official obligations, I leave the reader to decide.

When spring came, Judge E.F. Dyer returned to Lake County. Mr. Marion--whose escape from the mob, after having been run up by the neck, is given above---also returned, and swore out warrants before the judge for all who had taken part in the outrage. The culprits gathered all they could--nearly thirty men--and the sheriff with them, as he in character as well as ability was more in his element with a mob than anywhere else. They came with guns and pistols, and entered the courtroom armed. The judge ordered them to divest themselves of their arms, and they laid them off in the back-end of the court-

"The stream was running full knee-deep of slush...I waded across, wiping my feet as dry as I could with my handkerchief, got my boots on, and made four miles through the snow to Garro's Ranch."

house; after which their cases were called. Jesse Marion, the principal witness, and others, were not uninterested spectators while the crowd was gathering. From what they saw and heard they feared to go to the trail, and court was adjourned till eight o'clock the next morning for want of evidence. The judge slept over a store, with some others, and was told by the sheriff that he could not leave that night. Mr. Gilland was there. His mule was watched through the night, and without doubt, if he had attempted to get it, he would have been shot. He was advised to leave, and did so, slipping out over the hill, and walked to Fair Play, through the mountains, twenty-five miles, and reported the situation.

At eight o'clock court was called, and the accused were dismissed for lack of evidence. They all went out. Mr. Hayden stopped with the judge a minute. Some one called him down on purpose. He went, and as soon as he left, five men from the crowd went up the stairs at the back-end of the building. The judge was sitting in an office chair, and three or four shots were fired. One ball struck the chair, another went through his arm above the wrist, and on through the window. One man on the outside heard him cry: "Spare my life!" But he must have made toward them, and been caught by some of them near the door, as the pistol was evidently put close to his head---the hair being all burned around the bullet-hole, which was just behind his ear. They all went down the

steps, and mingled among their crowd, which was waiting for them at the foot of the stairs. A man looked through a crack, as it was a log house, and saw the tragedy, and was the first to reach him. But the judge never spoke, and breathed his last in a few minutes. Another man, Mr. Woodard, standing above on a bank, only a few feet away, saw them come out, and knew them all. He was imprudent enough to tell what he saw, and not long after was shot off his horse and killed. The man who shot him resumed his abode with the mob. It was called "self-defense." So it was--- to the mob.

An officer was called, an inquest held, a verdict rendered: That E.F. Dyer came to his death by unknown hands. The mob terrorized the community, for only about half their number were brought by a warrant; the rest came armed to prevent those accused from being tried. The inquest was virtually in the hands and interest of the mob.

One of their number was mysteriously shot several years after in his own store. I will narrate the circumstances as I heard them. He had a yound man hired to herd for him, said to have been a nephew of Mr. Harrington, the first man murdered in the annals of the mob. He came into the neighborhood some time after his uncle had been killed, and was heard to say that if he ever discovered his uncle's murderer, he would be avenged. After working for Mr.

Nathrop for some time, he quit, and went to the store to settle, and must have settled with Mr. Nathrop. He was the last one seen in the store before Mr. Nathrop's dead body was found lying on the floor. The young man rode to Buena Vista, a few miles distant, and danced most of the night, and in the morning left on the cars. A reward of several hundred dollars was offered for his arrest, but he has not been heard of since. He could easily have been taken; but the people feared that Gibbs was back, hunting his oppressors. The mob all feared Gibbs a great deal more than they did the devil, and so let the youth escape. Nathrop was the wealthiest man connected with the Lake County mob.

My son was murdered at eight o'clock A.M., July 3, 1875. The few people that were at Granite buried him in the usual place of interment, where there were a number resting. Among them was Brother Rufus Lumery, an itierant preacher, who preached to us at my house when Elias was four years old. But I was not satisfied to leave him among such a set of murderers. So, some three years after, my son Samuel and my son-in-law, C.C. Streetor, went with a wagon nearly one hundred and fifty miles, and removed his body to Bailey, Colorado, where they disinterred my father's remains, and bore both bodies to Castle Rock, Douglas County, and buried them side by side. I considered this our duty. But unless it were a duty, I would never do so

again, for the reason that it brings all the feelings of a father or a son back afresh. I learned by this experience that a metallic coffin does not last long. Father had been buried only six years, yet his metallic coffin was rusted full of holes. The other was pine, and sound. They opened it, and the corpse was natural---only a speck of mold on one cheek. God only knows how hard a trial this terrible tragedy was to me. After the lapse of all these years, the memory of it rushes over me like a flood. Yet I would infinitely rather endure my suffering than what his cruel murderers must have experienced. One was so crazed that he drowned himself. Another had what was called the "horrors," and finally miserably died. God's curse was upon them all. Be it so!...

I went back to Breckenridge, which shortly experienced a characteristic mining boom. A report was spread that about Breckenridge were immense bodies of gold quartz and carbonates, three feet deep. People of all classes came across the range, and, of course, the inevitable dance-house, with degraded women, fiddles, bugles, and many sorts of music, came too. There was a general hubbub from dark to daylight. The weary could hardly rest. Claims were staked out everywhere, and the prospector thought nothing of shoveling five feet of snow to start a shaft. Saloons, grocery-stores, carpenter-shops, and every kind of business sprang up, including stamp-mills and smelters.

All classes were excited beyond all good sense. Town-lots, that could have been bought before at twenty-five to fifty dollars, brought fifteen hundred dollars. Corrals, logheaps, and brush-thickets were all turned into town-lots. Those owning ground thought it worth ten times more than it was. The excitement was almost as great as when they thought the Indians were coming. The preacher thought it time to secure a lot for a church. He canvassed all the town; but none had a lot to give. One was offered away out, but was refused. Giving a back-lot for a church had played out with me. In the fall I bought a lot and a cabin. It was about one hundred and fifty feet deep by fifty wide. The Town Company undertook to change the survey and take about two-thirds of it from me under pretense that the county had a claim on it. They even undertook to fence it up; but when they began, I began too. I hired men to put in posts; but as soon as I turned by back they came to my men, within forty feet of my house, and told them they would send an officer and arrest them. My hands quit. After dinner I went to digging post-holes myself. The Town Company's representative came with two witnesses, and warned me to stop work. I never laid down my pick, but told him I was a man, and a law-abiding man at that, and his were as good witnesses as I wanted; and I warned him before them to keep off my lot and to leave. By this time the witnesses started, and he followed. He

was the company's commissioner; and was very good when he found he could not bulldoze me. I gave half my lot to the trustees to build a church on. We carried a subscription paper till I got enough to start on; and went to the saw-mills, got all the lumber I could, and we went to work and put up a house twenty-five by fifty feet, posts sixteen feet high, and inclosed it. I nailed the first shingle, and did more work on it than any other men.

While I went to conference and friends finished the roof and put the floor down; and the next Sunday we had service in the first church on the Western Slope in our conference, with a good organ...

In 1879...I returned to Brecken-ridge, where the boom had begun in March. In about a year most of the excitement in town-lots had passed over; and in eighteen months building had quit, and not long after a fire burned a block, and the camp went down. There has been no building since to speak of, and town-lots have gone back as fast as they went up.

As conference gave me no help, and the people but little---the members being poor---I put in all my time at work in some way. Being well acquainted with the mountains an mining, I was paid good wages for locating claims. When the snow was deep, I went on snow-shoes, always feeling that a preacher had a right to earn his living if he could not get it by preaching; but no right to leave his charge. I could preach three and four

times, and work three or four days in the week. If fact, I sometimes earned more by moonshine labors than I could by preaching. In the summer of this year my wife boarded some men, and helped in that way...

My practical knowledge, as before stated, made my services as a locater in demand. Sometimes I gave them to deserving young fellows, whom fortune has used roughly. Two such were Candell and Thompson. In the spring of 1880 they came to me for information. Snow was more than knee-deep. They were out of money, except enough to board them a few days, and put up a log pen, ten or twelve feet square, just large enough for them to stand up in and make a stopping-place. The next thing was a job of work. I was employed to sink holes on some claims, to hold them, and gave them employment. I bought tools for them, and we started up the mountains, I leading. Soon the trail gave out, and we broke a path in snow waist deep. We carried picks, shovels, tent, and blankets. It was hard climbing for the boys; but they said: "If that old man can get there, we must." And we did. I showed them where to dig. That day they had a shaft three feet deep, and slept in it at night.

They worked for some time, making fair wages---say three dollars per day---and then they and myself took up some ground in company. They also continued to work and prospect for themselves though the summer. Thompson found some float

mineral, and followed it up to where it came up to the grass roots, and sunk a hole on it ten feet deep, and threw out several hundred pounds of rich mineral, gray copper, worth five hundred dollars to the ton. He staked his claim---one hundred and fifty by one thousand five hundred feet. He did not know how rich it was, and let one Parkison have a fourth interest for one hundred dollars, and would have sold the balance for two hundred and fifty dollars, but his man failed to come to time. He kept the location a secret. I had not asked him where it was, but said: "You have got on my claim, I suspect." He replied: "You have no claim up there." I answered: "I prospected up there three years ago, and left by shovel to hold by claim." "Where is your claim?" he said. I inquired if he had been at the head of a certain ditch. "Yes," was his answer. "Well," I replied, "my claim crosses about thirty rods above that." "My claim," he said, "is not within three hundred feet of that."

I rode up, and found my shovel; and just up the hillside I saw his corner stake, and followed to his works. I was pleased with his show for a lode, and was glad for his sake. Seeing the ground was vacant on each side of his claim, before I left I staked one claim south and four north of it. Unable to do the work myself, I took two or three pieces of his ore home with me, and told an assayer where it came from, and that I had staked the ground adjoining; and as I had to attend to my

church building, proposed to let him go in with me, if he liked the show; he to do my work for an interest. He went, and was pleased, and we made a contract. He looked at Mr. Thompson's prospect, and wanting some one to do the work, I suggested Thompson, as he would want to keep an eye on his own claim. He said nothing about buying the claim. When Thompson came in to our house, I told him they wanted to see him; and knowing that he had offered his claim for two hundred and fifty dollars, advised him, if they wanted to buy him out, not to sell for nothing. My wife named a thousand dollars, as it was easier to fall than to raise. He went and asked them twelve hundred; but they offered him a thousand, ten per cent down, and the rest in sixty days. He returned in a few minutes with his hundred dollars, and said it was the first time he had ever had that much at once. Then they wanted to see Mr. Parkinson but told Thompson not to tell how he sold. Mrs. Dyer said: "You tell Mr. Parkinson to come here as he goes, and I will post him." He came, and then sold his fourth for five hundred dollars, ten per cent down. There were four of the company, and so they had the big thing, and---by doing the work agreed on---three-fourths of mine also.

The ore was very rich---from low grade to a thousand dollars a ton. But one of the parties assayed some of it, and showed me the certificate. It was so low that I never said a word to Mr.

Thompson about it. I was disappointed in it. If anybody knew it was rich, it was those who bought it. In a day it was all over the camp that the boys had been swindled, the ore being fabulouly rich. And, as a matter of course, the discoverers felt bad over the loss of a good thing. Everybody asked why they did not have it assayed. Because they had no money to pay on a risk, as but very few had received any benefit by the assays, and many considered it money out. Parties told them they were swindled, and that the sale could be set aside, and that on certain conditions they would have it done. What those conditions were I never knew. They were not to have anything except they could prove fraud, and so get the property back. So they went to law.

I has been asked by the assayer if I wished to have some of the Warrior's Mark ore assayed. I replied: "No; I have no interest in the lode." Afterwards he called me in and showed me his report on it, and it was lower than I had thought possible. I thought no more about it at the time, until after the sale. When they had me on the witness-stand, they questioned me as to the assay I had seen. I told them what I knew of it. "Did you tell either of the parties before the sale?" "No." "Why did you not tell them?" "Because I was taken back, and thought it would do them no good." This showed that they were not influenced by the assay. So the purchasers held the diggings, and the poor boys got no more.

"What a difference between then and now! Then, a half-beaten wagon-track on an Indian trail; now, the passenger sits on a cushioned seat, and rests at night in a sleeping-car!"

122

They were advised to compromise with the first party, but they would not.

Now the company go to work, but soon winter is on, and snow anywhere from five to eight feet deep. Some good mineral was raised; but the water was strong, and they concluded to sell. The price was put at three hundred thousand dollars for the whole, including my interest. I was to have eight thousand, five hundred. About the 1st of January, 1881, I began work on a log house. Had a good horse and sled, six miles away, at Breckenridge. Selected a place to build, and taking my horse, with chain and whiffle-tree, went eight rods, mid-sides in snow, and dragged in the first tree. And so, cutting and hauling logs, and going back home each day, returning to work in the morning with lumber, I finished my house. It was seventeen feet by seventeen, a story and a half in height, shingle roof, two floors, and doors. By the 19th of February I moved my wife and the last of our goods. By that time I had a hole against the bank in the snow to stable my horse. Laid poles on the snow, and put pine-brush for roof, and he was comfortable till his slab stable was built. We were within a half mile of the Warrior's Mark Lod e, which was the center of attraction for mining experts and speculators. Men would come, and look, and send experts; and then others would come. All wished to make money. Some would levy blackmail, under threats of spoiling

the sale. After all the efforts, the property was not sold.

The weather becoming good, they hired a superintendent and about fifty men, and resumed work. In six months they took out, as well as I could learn, between seventy-five and eighty thousand dollars. During this time, they stocked the property at three millions. After one dividend, it failed to pay any more for a time under the management. I took ten thousand dollars in stock for my part. At this time I began to look at the stock system, and concluded to let that be the last stock I would ever have anything to do with in mining. For these reasons: First, the amount is put at three times its worth; second, there are directors, clerks, and treasurer, president, superintendent, and bosses, all on pay, besides the hands. These, with mismanagement, wire-working, whisky, cards, and fancy women, beat the average lode. After several attempts to get pay out ot the mine, a man took the property to work. He had secured more than half the stock, and had the control. He bought mine. I realized two thousand dollars.

I have given this sketch to show some of the difficulties of prospecting, selling, or running a mine. Yet mining is the business of the country.